Right Place, Right Time

RIGHT PLACE, RIGHT TIME

RAYMOND PELEKAMOYO

WORDS by DESIGN

CONTENTS

Before you begin, allow me to first begin by saying that I am not a writer but an adventurous scribbler. Now, this is a little book about me and significant life events that make me who I am.

A book about guidance, relationships, and identity.

FOREWORD

Early in the year 2020, I had prayed and hoped to meet an individual who would inspire me. I had wished to meet a person that was kind and welcoming, someone that made the people around them feel better about themselves, but more importantly, I wanted to meet someone whose brain I could peek into. It was on a Sunday night, an event which was sold to me as a 'welcome party', when I met a broken-legged man who would fit that description. When he told me the story of how he had broken his leg, I was disinterested. In the back of my mind, he was just another one of those foreign, flamboyant types that wanted everybody's attention – and I wasn't going to give him mine. However, that changed when he called me 'king'. With just one word he made me feel important, and I started to pay attention. I rarely meet people that affect me in the way that his energy did. I did not know exactly what it was about him, but I was convinced that I needed to get to know him. Meeting him that night, and the interactions that followed, confirmed that I had received my blessing. In him I saw someone I could learn life from, and someone that uplifts and brings people together. On that Sunday night, I met Raymond Pelekamoyo.

Wazani Muwezwa

NATHAN'S STORY

My name is Nathan Owens. I'm a US Marine and I've had the fortune to travel the world many times over, both in the military and throughout my adolescence.

I first met Raymond during my time as a US Marine in London. Marines are the ambassadors of America you don't hear about. We are silent professionals. We guard personnel, entries, and most importantly the secrets of the US Embassies around the world. An unspoken part of the job is socialising and connecting with the wider community wherever we are based. One of the benefits is that we regularly host parties at our bases with guests admitted by name invites only. Raymond, being a good friend of the Marines, was of course invited to one of my first parties, which led to us being introduced through a mutual friend. He instantly got my attention and won me over. I could tell we had a lot in common.

Little did I know at the time, but I was a 'third culture kid' (Raymond introduced me to these concepts later). We didn't get into the details of our backgrounds at the time of the party, but in that short interaction, I could already tell that we would be lifelong friends.

Our next interaction was an unexpected one, but it was the one that changed the way I viewed the world. It sealed the deal for me. We went to the Wireless Festival in London, and if you have ever been to a summer music festival, you know the energy they have. It's hot, the lines are long, and there are people at the entry already too intoxicated to join the venue. There's the smell of food, humans and utter chaos in the air. All this together sounds horrible, but add music and now you can have a good time! This festival was one of the best I've ever been to.

One thing that I noticed about Raymond was that he never shied away from an opportunity to network. He kept telling women that I was a secret spy, accompanied by a select few photos of me in uniform. The most important aspect of this interaction was that we got to know each other much more and talked about the concept of third culture kids.

At one point we found a spot to sit down and have a break from being sandwiched between the waves of people. Whilst eating, Raymond and I talked about all the places we had traveled to. It was interesting to know that we both had traveled the world and had a tonne of individual experiences. However, after visiting and living in so many countries, when it came to the question, 'Where are you from?', we both had the same feeling. I wouldn't call it a feeling of disgust or annoyance, but rather a feeling of confusion. When you've lived in many countries, you grow in many countries. For most people, when they describe where they are from, the basic underlying idea is a safe place where you can lay your head, with family and friends that love and appreciate you for who you are. Most importantly, in my opinion, it's where you grow and gain your values. We had both found ourselves in various countries making meaningful connections with people indistinguishable from family – we felt safe there, and those places have molded us and given us the values in life that we live by. In the words of the upcoming preface, this way of development "leaves you wondering where home is." This mutual understanding of being nomads and only calling a place 'home' because we were born there opened up an entirely different conversation between us.

As you continue reading, Raymond will explain how this conversation that occurs naturally between third culture kids – how we relate and use the various skills that we have learned through our lives, and most importantly, how we use those experiences to bring value and make connections wherever we're planted. If you're a third culture kid, and you also have a passion to travel the world, embrace where your home is today. When someone asks you, "Where are you from?", it's okay to tell them you're a citizen of the world. Your home is the earth and your love for people and culture serves as a reminder to the world – borders are just references.

Charles, Prince of Wales. Donald Trump, 45th President of the United States, Melanie Trump, Nathan Owens (far right)

PREFACE

The open and interconnected world we encompass has been one that has allowed development to happen at a speed that we could never have imagined. In recent decades citizens of the world have had the opportunity to cross borders with ease. Children born into this environment are known as 'third culture kids (TCK)' or 'Global Nomads' and are considered culturally distinct. These children are the children of the world, ambassadors of their many homes.

This book was written through the eyes of many third-culture kids. It will allow you to see why they are astonishingly unique individuals. We are shaped from a young age to see the world through small lenses that we call eyes. Our senses are put through their limits as we begin to explore at a young age what life is all about. As months turn into years, we are faced with the reality that we have been exposed to so many experiences on a global scale that we only yearn for more. There are a few that have had the opportunity (or curse, depending on how this book navigates your thought process) to see so much of this world at a young age – like myself, a young wanderer with little control over my own global footprint. The son of a Zambian tennis player and rebellious air hostess, who would have thought the actions of two young spontaneous wanderers in love would lead to a young man sitting in his bedroom staring at a map wondering where home was, with hundreds of pieces of himself scattered across the globe. Many had the answers I've been dearly searching for.

So, for me to be open enough to uncover the truth in my life, I must be able to transport you to distinct chapters of my life, memories of my life that will tell stories that relate to many other global nomads.

For my entire life I have always been 'on the go'. If you allow me, I'll try my best to take you back to a time where my life was located in a completely different culture to where I am today. I will create a significant timeline throughout this journey and together we will uncover what it means to be a 'third culture kid.'

Many are not aware that we are 'third culture children', a sociological concept that I have used as a description of myself since I was young. This book is an explosion of thoughts, a collection of stories and conversations with other third culture kids. I attempt to dive deep into the behaviours and psychological characteristics that define and ultimately make us so different.

My hope is that readers of this book can take something from this book that will help them question and understand who they are. This book has been written with honest reflection and transparency about myself as an acting being. I am an agent of my own thoughts and the words written have been carefully chosen to give the most accurate reflections of pinpoints on my personal timeline.

You might be a global nomad reading this, or you might actually not relate at all. That's fine, you have your own experiences to share. That's the beauty of uncovering the life of a third culture kid.

CHAPTER ONE

"I am not from a place. I am from people."

"Where are you from?"

"Here we go again," is echoed in my mind. I've never mentioned this response before, because I don't get asked that question very often, but, uh, I'm in a bit of a pickle to be honest. The idea of answering this question rings alarm bells as I begin to think about which location would best summarize who I am feeling at that exact moment. I know only a few people might find this question confusing or scary. It's simple enough really, isn't it? Four simple words that we have grown up with our entire life. What could possibly go wrong? There are just a couple of simple descriptions that we have grown up with since birth:

"Who are you?" "Where do you come from?"

Two simple, but very confusing questions. To my three brothers and myself, it really isn't that easy. Such questions would usually first evoke a huge sigh and then a three-minute-long explanation. For the purpose of this book, allow me to introduce myself. My name is Raymond Pelekamoyo, born in Zambia, more specifically in Lusaka, the capital city. I am on paper a British citizen and in Zambia I am not recognised at all as Zambian because of my lack of ability to speak the local languages. Before you judge me, let me just remind you that in Zambia there are around 72 tribes and over 70 different languages! At the age of five, I moved to Harare in Zimbabwe until I was eight years old. I then relocated to the United Kingdom to a small but quirky city called Oxford. Now, to save you time, I'll skip the details and just inform you that every single one of my brothers by blood is born in a totally different country. Yes, I know, this is the fortune of always being on the go!

So as you can see, my life was designed in a very unorthodox way. I had an unconventional upbringing. I am a third culture kid and I am very proud, angry, jittery, and happy about being one. For the unfamiliar and uninitiated, third-culture kids (those who have spent considerable time in another culture) are those who have created a third culture that is their own. As a result, they can be self-questioning and protective about their surroundings.

Relocating to Oxford was a fantastic opportunity and a significant chapter in my life. I had great expectations of my life here – I had been daydreaming about this fascinating place on the way to England and indulged in all the British TV shows and sports to prepare myself. On the flight to England, I would picture in my head the language, music and what the food would be like. Believe it or not, I thought that England had yellow American school buses and the greenest neighbourhoods you could imagine.

However, when we arrived at our new home, I was taken aback by the size of the property which was much smaller than I had imagined. It's funny how I was completely wrong and mismanaged my expectations, but I can laugh at it now when I look back.

For example, the night before my first day at school I didn't sleep much, but I remember ironing my clothes and placing them on the bottom of my bunk – I had my school clothes and shiny leather shoes that I had carried all the way from Zimbabwe. They were by far the most dapper items of my entire outfit. Looking back, I must have looked like a 40-year-old midget in his Sunday best! You see, in Zimbabwe it was a requirement to dress smartly in the appropriate school uniform. However, the school I went to in Oxford didn't have a school uniform – red flag!

As I arrived at my new school (extra early, may I add), I was greeted at the classroom by my new teacher. She was a young woman in her twenties with golden strawberry blonde hair wearing the brightest maxi dress which had little images of flowers. She was a very flimsy-looking woman, but straight away she pointed out how smart I looked, so I politely thanked her for before taking my seat. We ran through the usual introductions, and then she asked me what I wanted to be called. "Raymond Pyo Pyo Pelekamoyo, if you don't mind." You see, Raymond was my name given at birth. Pelekamoyo is my surname. 'Pyo Pyo' was the name given to me by my grandfather on my father's side. I was proud of my name. I felt that there was nothing left but my name to reflect my home. I clarified that my surname was spelled "P-E-L-E-K-A-M-O-Y-O."

Suddenly, BASH! There was a loud noise as the classroom door flew wide open and there was a stampede of footsteps . I could hear all the children laughing and running into the classroom. Voices merged into one sound, with the children shouting at the top of their lungs. Then I noticed a trend – they were all dressed in their everyday clothes, some even in sports kits. My first blunder had been to totally misunderstand the dress policy. Thankfully the teacher reassured me with a kind smile.

"Class, we have a new student today. I would like you to meet Raymond."

I stood up and stared at my new class, but pulled a confused face at everyone... the teacher had completely missed out on my other two names. My heart sank. However, I still signed my name badge with 'Pyo Pyo'. One way or another I was going to make it known to everyone who I was. Call this my red flag number two.

When I put it on my chest, straight away I received the funniest looks and confused questions. The result? I was nicknamed 'Pinocchio'. This made me realise that the teacher had not in fact forgot to mention my full name, but was trying to protect me by making it easier for me. After realising what was happening, I removed the badge and created a new one with just 'Raymond'. As I placed the badge back on my chest, I heard two melodic voices in front of me asking, "Where are you from Raymond?" I lifted my head from my chest and stared up at these two identical shaved-headed white twin brothers, both wearing the exact same grey and blue tracksuits. Before answering I thought carefully. I quickly evaluated my actions from the time I had arrived until that very moment. I gathered my strength, took a deep breath, and whispered in a controlled voice, "America". At that moment, I knew my life was going to get a whole lot more complicated.

After being at my new school for a few months, picking up new behaviours and 'lingo' became second nature to me. I felt comfortable and being known as the new 'American kid' was pretty cool. All I ever did was retell the stories my mother had told me about her experiences living in America.

Education was never one of my strong points, and in Zimbabwe, if you had missed a single assignment, you would have to stand alongside the instructor with a broad or thorny stick. However, the ban on corporal punishment had come into force in British state schools in 1986, so I was thrilled when I discovered I had been awarded detention that entailed writing an apology on a Post-it note. I laugh now when I look back at it!

Good things in England were beginning to happen to me, and before I knew it, I was heading back to Zambia to spend some time with family. When I found out that I could share my experiences with my friends and family and play with friends in my old neighborhood again, I was elated. However, it came as a total surprise to me that nobody there understood why I was so excited about my new life in England. My friends found it difficult to follow my conversations, and although working together on our football skills was also fun, it had become entirely different for me. Kids on the street teased me for dressing and speaking the way I did. They laughed at me because I wore sneakers when I played football. As I neared my grandparent's home, I had to dry my eyes because I had been weeping for the whole journey. That was when I realised that this wasn't where I belonged. Life was changing.

Returning to their homeland also causes travellers to feel an opposite culture shock. The longer the immigrant stays in their new country, the more likely it is that they will have trouble dealing with culture shock returning to their home country. People with severe culture shock are reported to have high stress, depression, anxiety, and social isolation. Being a third culture kid you can appreciate how vast the universe is… but still be lonely.

Raymond in Oxfordshire, 2001

CHAPTER TWO

Even the best dads make mistakes.
But there is no mistaking their love for their children.

I wouldn't say I got along well with my father as a kid. We didn't grow up with the traditional father-son relationship, but we were connected by our love of tennis, our willingness to venture out into the world, and competition. It was a very 'coached' childhood, in fact tennis seemed to be my only destiny.

My father was from the Nsenga people of Zambia, a proud Zulu tribe that was part of my father's lineage, a tribe that was familiar with Zambia and Mozambique. The Bantu-speaking Nsenga people also inhabited the Luangwa River valley area of south-eastern Zambia, located in two districts of Eastern Province, Nyimba and Petauke (my father's district and also formally mine). About 700,000 people identify themselves as Nsenga disciples, part of a known family language group called Bemba.

I've never written my family history before, but this is where my family comes in. On my mother's side, the Bemba tribe migrated into Zambia from the Luba Kingdom. Interestingly enough, both the Bemba and Nsenga people migrated from the Luba Kingdom, Kola to be specific, during the Bantu Migration, which took place between the fifteenth and seventeenth centuries. Legend has it that the chief of the Luba tribe, Mukulumpe, married a woman named Mumbi Lyulu Mukasa who was of the crocodile clan (known as the Ng'andu clan). She had three sons called Chiti, Nkole, and Katongo, who fled the Luba kingdom following a dispute. They took with them their followers and their sister Chilufya.

In order to expand their kingdom, the Bemba raided smaller tribes, taking their land, resources, and women. Nkole and Chiti eventually died and were buried at Mwalule, which is now a royal burial ground where all Bemba chiefs (addressed as Chitimukulu) are buried. Chilufya's son was crowned the new chief, starting a matrilineal form of royal succession that continues to this day. The Bemba eventually settled in present-day Northern Province after they spotted a dead crocodile which they took to be a good omen.

My mother was Bemba and was as stubborn as a mule! In fact, she read this book and looked at me with a straight face and said, "Raymond, you haven't mentioned that Bemba women are the head of their tribe. We are fierce and independent." I told you she was stubborn! When my mother was younger, she went out of her way to do the opposite of what was expected of her. Nothing for her was ever effortless. She was the sister of sixteen other siblings, who from eldest to youngest were: Bwalya (named after my mum's father), Bwalya (named after my mum's mother's father), Mukuka, Maureen (my mum), Mubanga, Chishimba (named after my mum's father's mother); then my grandparents divorced after which came Bwalya (repeated again, but we call him Derek), Dean, Chishimba, Katundu, Mwene, Kafula, Simon, Mwango, Chewe, Chanda, Chonta, and Patience.

Mum was born in Kasama, Zambia, raised in Brussels, Belgium, and later moved to Washington DC in the United States, where she went to school before escaping to return back to Zambia to train as an air hostess. I recall when I was young being glued to the dining table listening to my mother tell stories about her childhood. She talked about the countries she visited, her family and wanting to be an air hostess with her best friend, which consequently led to her leaving college in America and rebelling against her father. She didn't know when to stop – there was no telling her otherwise.

At the time Zambia was one of the best countries in the world to visit for adventure tourism; in 1988 it was honoured with the nickname 'Zambia: Scenery and Wildlife Capital of the Continent', with one of the world's natural wonders, the beautiful Victoria Falls. This brief promotional description of Zambia may seem biased, but I kid you not, it is as beautiful as all the Google images you may find. In addition, the capital city was attracting numerous business people and their families from all over the world, many of whom were new to this part of the world, many some returning.

It was a thrilling time to be a young person. When he was younger, my father had not yet found his niche. With thirteen brothers and sisters, he was the son of a kind and gentle Zambian man, the brother to nine other siblings (from eldest to youngest, we have Flavius, Winfrida, Jennifer, Bernard, Patricia, Maureen, Victor – my father – Gerald, Constance, and Brenda).

My father followed in the footprints of his father's Management Accountancy practice. There was never a moment when he was utterly content in this world. The recollection I am about to tell you comes from my uncle, who held back tears as he told this story around a fireplace on the day of my father's traditional burial in Zambia in 2011.

I recall Ba Vic being street smart. He would only want others to be happy and give everyone a chance to see the world. When we were in school, we never had much income. We usually went to the shops on Friday, had a drink, and chilled at someone's place, it was all very simple. A routine. However, once we stepped foot in the store, something interesting invariably happened. Victor was buying everyone snacks and food. There's no way we could ever afford that. Victor still kept his debts. As the weeks rolled by, we began to suspect him of doing something illegal. On Friday mornings, he would be the first to leave for his chores, which started at 5.00 am. So, we hatched a scheme to keep tabs on him throughout the early hours of the morning. It must be said that we never knew when he got up that morning, so we stayed in our car all night. He appeared on his doorstep at 5.00 am wearing his navy tracksuit and carrying a big rectangle-shaped bag. We were now wholly perplexed. What could he possibly be up to? What is in that bag? So many questions to ask.

I saw him enter a posh building in the city of Lusaka. Now, we were terrified. I approached the building from the rear and proceeded at a snail's pace. He had stunned us into silence. I could not believe what I was seeing, like the others. An elite 20 man upper-class tennis club. Victor began doing an energizing warm-up exercise at the head of the line. We had found Victor teaching tennis to some of the elite diplomats and businessmen. Naturally, this is where I find my interest in tennis. Victor helped me improve my game and provided the coaching I needed and consequently, I became Zambia's number 1 tennis player.

When the final words were spoken, a hush settled over the camp. The group released a breath of appreciation. But then, how did an accountant from a lower-class family become engaged to be an air hostess? My eyes were fixed on my uncle and my mouth was wide open, and if I didn't stop myself, the words would just tumble out. So, he carried on with his story.

> When I was at my peak playing tennis, everyone and all types of organisations were fighting to have myself and Victor train them at the sport. We were excited about one organisation in particular. It was a crew of five beautiful young women, Air Zambia female flight attendants. I remember this day so vividly, because it was when I first met your mother. She was the current Miss Zambia Air and it was obvious she was the 'IT' girl. My job was to train with her while the other coaches and players trained the rest of them. Before stepping onto the court, your father pulled me aside. He pleaded with me to swap, as he felt that she was the love of his life. I hesitantly agreed and I guess the rest is history.

I strongly believe that before I was brought into the picture, the various pieces seem to have been preordained. I've always known I was destined to be a nomad. However, I've always tried to associate myself with other people from an early age and manage to communicate profoundly with others because I attempt to understand their true character.

I became more convinced of the meaningfulness of life after my father died. I've never really reflected on grief or dived into my thoughts surrounding the emotive behaviours that one may experience. I understand grief may differ between individuals. I'm not saying all TCKs experience the same emotions in the same way. However, there are some similarities in the way we face challenges head-on. We design ourselves to move forward, not to slow down and take stock of what has passed. So for me, it was as though my father had never been sick. Sounds crazy, doesn't it?

Becoming a third-culture kid can be a curse, yet with a sprinkling of beautiful flowers. While you may be fearful of flying so high, you are cushioned by the excitement of the unknown.

Third Culture Kids tend to move, not because of necessity, but because of habit. This is what I had experienced throughout my life, and it became ingrained in me.

The Culture Trip. 2018. An Introduction to Zambia's Bemba Tribe. [online] Available at: <https://theculturetrip.com/africa/zambia/articles/an-introduction-to-zambias-bemba-tribe/> [Accessed 15 October 2021].

Victor Pelekamoyo on the left, Maureen Bwalya in the middle, Lighton Musonda (Zambia's number one tennis player) at Lusaka Tennis Club

CHAPTER THREE

Do you know what a foreign accent is? It's a sign of bravery.
Those are people who crossed an ocean to come to this country.

Amy Chua

For those who have moved to other countries and now call that country your home, you may consider yourself to be 'ex-pats' or 'global nomads'. You've come to accept that you're a foreigner in your new home, but that isn't the case with us. I, for example, was born in a beautiful place called Lusaka, in sub-Saharan Africa. A beautiful place I immediately fell in love with. Even though I was very young, I can still vividly remember my childhood and the music that moulded my eardrums and shaped my brain in such a way to be able to easily pick up and understand languages I encounter.

Many would find the art of juggling or kicking a ball around as being very easy, but for me hearing words from another country and trying to remember what they mean was my skill – a skill that I still use today when I need to impress or connect deeply with people. I saw my ability to pick up languages as a beautiful gift, handed to me by the god of semantics. At the same time, this multi-lingual talent can also cause a lot more stress – you have to be able to fit into many different cultures all at once, which causes anxiety and presents challenges when it comes to maintaining that level of communication.

This unusual behaviour became clear to my parents as I experienced many different places and schools. Being surrounded by friends from different communities around the world, I was able to understand conversations and describe what was going on to my parents effortlessly. They might have been in awe, but they had experienced this previously in countries we had lived in before.

So, once again I began to shapeshift myself into a new character each time. I started to resemble a character from 'X-Men' with the curse of not knowing where I belonged. The longer I stayed in an environment I had been placed in, my ears would start to deceive me and I would begin to question what language I was translating during conversations. Surely I wasn't the only one who felt this alone? I couldn't possibly be the little odd tomato among the ripe bunch. Just as in the comic books, where the X-men all had their battles, longing to search for those that resembled them, those who would be their role models when their own personal roles were being questioned.

However, away from the fantasies of the flying beasts and the shooting eyes, I faced my own challenge. I couldn't find a person who looked like me. If I had been a believer in statistics, I would have been much more confident, as amongst all of the billions of living organisms I could not be alone. And if you're wondering… that's correct, we are not alone at all. In fact, in recent years we have started coming out of our shadows and representing who we are – showing the world that we are lost in translation, yet proud of our global passport.

There is, for example, an Afro-buttered boy, born to a Kenyan father and mother who spent his developmental years in Hawaii and Indonesia. He sounds familiar I hope... he is in fact the world's most popular third culture boy, former President Barack Obama. So the third culture kids got their 'Xavier', the genetically engineered superhero who came to save the day in 2008 when Barack Obama was elected as the 44th President of the United States.

The world nomad ideal was utterly embodied in Barack after his time spent in Indonesia during infancy. When we first encountered the young Barack, we were all impressed by his calm, smooth and sharp tongue. I can confidently say that no one was certain what to think about him, and people certainly didn't see him as one of the leaders of the free world. Something never added up about Barack Obama, and we all sensed it. He wasn't like any other American, and you always felt there was another layer to him that he never let revealed. He didn't look like every other American, and he certainly wasn't the image that the founding fathers had envisioned.

> I learned to slip back and forth between my black and white worlds, understanding that each possessed its language and customs and structures of meaning, convinced that with a bit of translation on my part the two worlds would eventually cohere. – Barack Obama*

The way Obama describes his experience is cold and chilling, to say the least. It's as if he is in touch with each and everybody, looking for a culture, while remaining a stranger and building an identity from past pieces. His writing transports people into a world that makes sense with their ideas.

What about me? Well, to me, my soul feels relaxed when I'm in England and surrounded by fellow Africans, especially Zambians and Zimbabweans. I feel at home somehow, but I also feel 'lost in translation'. I feel agitated, like a newly-passed driver stopped at a red light. I feel stirred as my mind instinctively translates conversations, but I cannot handle the words to be able to answer. Such circumstances and events need a degree of control, and sometimes I suddenly feel like a stranger when I have no control. I know that in many cultures, especially those with cultural stigma built into them, differences amongst young children were not welcomed. I was still vulnerable to abuse or rhetorical questions about my origins, because I had no choice but to speak English.

Origins are an essential aspect of your life in African culture. Many people consider themselves traitors if they do not remember their origins or have substantial evidence for them. As language is a large part of your history, many may call your loyalty into question if the language does not match the history.

Due to the long summer vacations, I became transfixed by my television for four weeks. I remember a scene from 'Roots' and I could not believe my eyes. An enslaved African man called Kunta Kinta was abducted in the eighteenth century, trafficked along the 'Middle Passage'. Thousands of Africans had been taken out of their homes and shipped to America. Europeans then visited Africa and captured Africans, like Kunta Kinta, using weapons that many Africans had never seen before. The sequences in the film make the viewer feel physically sick, witnessing the sheer manpower that was used to displace people around the world.

During the first two episodes of Roots, identity is identified as an important topic. Kunta Kinte and his family are obliged to recognise the names of slaves and to abandon many of their culture's essential customs and traditions. This leads to resistance among the slaves who need to preserve their identity, whilst also still seeking independence. The philosophy surrounding the value of identity was prominent in the film, regardless of where someone was in the world.

Identity is consolidated with pride in language. Language is so critical that it has become our most reliable communication portal.

This is an essential part of human development, a critical step towards our species' growth, and a way of communicating beyond our embodied selves. Language has, in a way, become the gateway to the minds of those that surround us, giving us a quick glimpse into another person's parallel universe. Language is the ultimate basis for our species' success.

And yet language has also become one of our species' most significant obstacles, with all of its ability to bind us and confuse our understanding as we try to understand and see the world through another's eyes.

TCKs are the world's civilization. Which language you speak or the cultures you have followed to your Third Home doesn't matter – although we come from all over the globe, we all come from the same creation. All TCKs are members of a culture which unites them as world thinkers and worldly, neutral admirers. However, the words we say and read can also isolate us from each other.

We tend to take these places with us everywhere we go, and they often become mythical because by and large we left them for good. The idea of building an identity is peculiar and fraught with a feeling of irrevocable loss. This identity can also be very insulating, and it is a non-external identity that affects people of all colours, ideologies, and skin accents. It is almost impossible to adequately explain in casual conversation.

We are akin to a minority, but one so tiny and dispersed that we have no coherent political constituency and are almost never reflected in mainstream culture. It is the type of condition which makes me internalise and want to write, because everything is invisible – everything is internal and ultimately limited to memory.

CHAPTER FOUR

I would rather walk with a friend in the dark, than alone in the light.

Hellen Keller

These children (Third Culture Kids) are losing the worlds they love, over and over. I believe from experience that these kids go through the same experiences as someone experiencing grief. They share the same patterns and behaviours; they put up walls; they burn bridges; and their emotions bubble out.

When my father died, I was in my first year of university and in the fifth new location that I would call home for the time being. When I received the news of my father's death, I felt my world crumble into a million pieces, each piece representing every memory that I had once shared with him. What was even more painful was that I had just started to belong again, finding my identity again, simply to have it then ripped away from me.

At my family home in Oxford, we conducted our traditional grieving process with British family and friends. During this time, I came across a photo album from my time in Zimbabwe which contained a photo that instantly took me back to my time in Harare.

In this photo, I am sitting next to a short Indian boy who looked rather upset – I'll explain later why he looked upset. He was called Roshi and was my best friend in Harare. I could say he was the 'bestest' friend in the whole world at that point of my life. Roshi was a quiet Indian boy who had migrated to Zimbabwe during the mining industry boom with his two Indian parents. We lived in a tall high-rise block surrounded by local Zimbabweans. Roshi and I both wanted to learn the local language, Shona, but the only time we ever spoke Shona was when ordering our favourite ice-cream from the van that pulled up before David Livingstone School, our primary school. I liked Roshi because he thought quickly on his feet, and he had a plan to only learn three phrases that would have been enough to get through the next few years of school.

Unobva Kupi
Where are you from?

Iri Kuita mari
How much?

Ndokwanisa Kuwana ice cream here?
Can I get ice cream?

Of course, the plan never succeeded, and funnily enough we had to learn the local language quickly. All over Harare we were always being asked endless questions about our origins, but we were just two five-year-old boys in a random world, compelled to take on a new culture.

Over time, we became very self-righteous Zimbabweans. We moulded our accents, and Shona rolled quickly off of our tongues – we could even order two ice-creams easily and tell the ice-cream man to keep the change!

26

However, one day something happened after school that immediately reminded us that we were not one of them (Zimbabwean) . I remember it was 4.00 pm, and Roshi and I were waiting for our mothers to come and pick us up from school. We usually ran back home and raced each other, and I'd normally win, but this time I felt generous and wanted Roshi to win to I slowed my speed to let him take over. His smile was unbelievable, from ear to ear, but it didn't last long as a grey, dusty Volvo suddenly hit Roshi at full speed. I stopped and felt the tears roll down my face. I couldn't believe it. I was crying because, in all honesty, I knew for sure that I would get my ass spanked by my mother. After all, I was foolish and careless.

What happened next caught everyone by surprise. The Volvo driver sprung out of his car and pleaded with Roshi's mother: "That's my fault. Madam, I am so sorry. Please don't report me. I'll pay for any medical bills." Who did he think we were? I yelled at the top of my voice, "Wapota watiuraya (You almost killed us)" before he was able to finish. Surprised, he looked up at me – he certainly didn't think that we were Zimbabweans – we did not look like we were.

Who really was I?

Let that question sink in for a second. It's only in moments like that when you realise that although we spend our lives planting seeds all over the world, yet our tree has no foundation. Rebecca Grappo, one of the most fascinating education and attachment experts in this field and an educational consultant specialising in children's placement, believes that there are three basic requirements: belonging, acceptance and relationships. For TCKs, each step to a new location removes these essential needs. Being powerless in decisions about their future, their numerous 'defeats' are often not recognised by their parents who make the decision to move, and this vital issue is untold, unknown, and rejected.

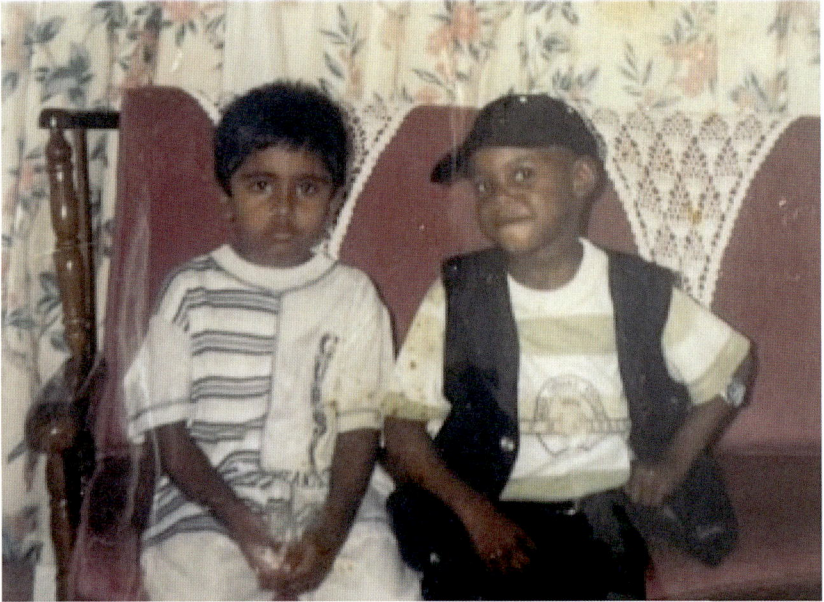

Roshi (left) Raymond Pelekamoyo (right) 1998, Harare, Zimbabwe

CHAPTER FIVE

"You keep me safe, I'll keep you wild."
Tiq and Kim Katrin

For my entire life I have managed to embody the philosophy of 'now', ensuring that my awareness is completely centred on the here and now. Do not worry about the future or think about the past – when you live in the now, you are living where life is happening. We live in the now. We want to know who you are and not what you are. For TCKs, once a relationship is over, we never keep in contact because of constantly moving forward.

The concept of 'living in the now' or 'being in the present' has its roots in eastern philosophies, but has gained popularity in mainstream western thinking in recent years thanks to the writings of people such as Eckhart Tolle and others. In this fast-paced and ever-changing digital world that we live in, there's a clear misdirection that has made us believe that we have actually become *more* connected to each other than before.

I sat through a psychology keynote speech in London in 2015 where I remember a fairly short doctor speaking who he ended his talk by reiterating that the more interconnected we become, the more lonely we make ourselves. This statement has never been truer for global nomads, who spend their whole lives travelling and meeting so many people that they never really find their true sense of belonging. It leaves an empty space that aches to be filled deep inside.

I believe, and I write this on paper as a statement, that TCKs' psychological makeup is different from others. Our posterior cingulate cortex (part of the brain that makes snap decisions about others) has been engineered in a way so as not use or base decisions purely on emotive reasoning. I once came across a graph that correlated the relationships people made with others. It showed how people focus their attention on creating bonds with people – that's their drive when they meet new people. However, when it comes to TCKs, their focus is not primarily on bonding with people – no, their drive is creating bridges instead. Creating bonds isn't a priority, due to their ever-changing lives and early upbringing.

Before I continue, it's important for me to be transparent and as honest as I can be while writing this chapter. My built-in response system has been engineered in such a way to flight instead of fight when a relationship with the other sex is falling apart. Ever since I was young, I was so used to not forming lasting relationships because I was always travelling. I taught myself to shut off certain emotions arising from a break in relationships. As global nomads, it is said that TCKs are limited in our capacity to fully invest in our local surroundings, that we have no sense of urgency to share and really care about what is going on. Our failure to deeply connect with others is so evident, but we brush it off.

One characteristic of being a TCK in a relationship is our need to be spontaneous. We need to not plan but rather be in the present. We have an urgency to do things today, not tomorrow, because out of everyone we know best that tomorrow things can change – in the same way that our bags are always packed and we are off to the next destination. Many of my friends fail to understand why I think this way.

I can now see that my inability to stand still has crippled most of my past relationships. This means that I am unable to comprehend growing and staying with one person – its not something I have ever done. This process of barrier-forming became evident to me in my past relationship, in fact, during my longest ever relationship. For the sake of the story, let's call her Amy. Amy was someone with whom I created a stable bridge when I had moved to my fifth location. She was someone I could relate to, as she loved to travel and was in a new place herself. I enjoyed where our relationship was going because it flowed without force. It was in some way spontaneous.

The day I realised that being a TCK would require a lot of rewiring was when Amy and I travelled to Barcelona. We sat in our hotel room, and she asked me what our plans were for the future. Without hesitation and thought I quickly answered, "I'm not sure, I haven't thought of you in my future, I just want to be with you in the now." As you read my words, you probably had the same facial expression that she had. I had utterly mucked that up! In my desire to be transparent I had treated Amy like all my other past broken friendships. In the most romantic yet unromantic way, I had told her that I wasn't sticking around. Of course, I didn't mean it, although part of me knew that I was going to leave.

So, these periodic cycles of separation and saying good-bye led me to develop certain methods of self-protection and avoidance to protect me from even more separation pain.

However, it's not unusual for TCKs to feel that their lives are beyond their own control. "You're left feeling utterly powerless about the direction your life is taking," says Sophie, another friend of mine who is a TCK, an Irish immigrant living in Kenya. She went on to explain that the unpredictability and instability of expatriate life causes many TCKs to stop looking forward to upcoming events – the announcement of the next move will probably upset all their plans. "I do find it hard to make lasting commitments," Sophie confesses. "Every plan I make for the future feels like a promise I'm going to break."

TCK relationship patterns demonstrate that they feel an urgency to make new friends wherever they go. They quickly shuffle through the standard get-to-know-you questions and then ask follow-up questions. This way they can paint a mental picture of where this person comes from. They don't fuss around long before moving on to deeper, more personal, conversations.

Personally, I often feel that there is never enough time to develop a particular relationship, so I like to dive right in. What other cultures may label as 'rude' and too nosy, is to me perfectly reasonable. If I can't connect with someone and move past the small talk quickly, I may lose interest. Why waste time on small talk? In most cases, almost anyone can be an instant friend to me.

As previously mentioned, our desire to live in the now has been ever more embodied in this global ecosystem that we pass through. This philosophy has been prominent in the teachings of Zen Buddhism. Zen has a distinctive characteristic, stressing the importance of the present moment. In our western relationship to time, this present moment becomes a minute sliver on the clock between an immense past and an endless future, in which we compulsively look back to the past to learn its lessons, and then project into a hypothetical future in which to apply these lessons. However, Zen is more about recovering and extending the current moment more than anything else.

Seeing any stranger as a possible new friend baffles my non-TCK friends. They argue that I trample all over the 'right approach' to a friendship and wear my heart on my sleeve too much. "Why are you always connecting with some stranger like that. Don't you have enough friends?" they ask. However, I think that because I connected with 'some stranger' on a deeper level, this quick relationship can become a life-long friend. And the concept of having enough friends does not apply because, by default, sooner or later it's time to once again say, "Peace out and take care."

FOOD FOR THOUGHT: THE EXPOSE GAMBLE

In fact, I've been told that I do wear my heart on my sleeve. By always having to find new friends, knowing that we won't have too long in the same city, I discovered my style of choosing friends: the exposé gamble. I am quick to spill my secrets to a new person, which makes me very vulnerable, something I like. Being vulnerable allows you to get to the centre of meaningful human experiences and demonstrates that I want to invest in a new friendship. To this day, I am amazed by how often I receive a confession in return, followed by a big smile. The relationship then develops quickly from there on and a new friendship blooms.

I've only ever been caught off guard once in my entire life, not being able to take a gamble at the fear of exposing my flaws. Coincidentally, this occurred with the opposite sex, and what was supposed to be a regular routine turned into a rollercoaster of emotions with butterflies in my stomach.

In the end, however, what I glorified as independence was actually a form of detachment. This type of indifference can cause a stinging pain of loneliness far greater than anything else.

CHAPTER SIX

Grief is the only time a TCK stays still long enough to feel the heart ache.

My people, no goodbyes to you
I'm just going to say good night
Right now, I can see it so vivid
Like it was just yesterday like I could relive it
Me and my grandparents on a field trip
And I'm the little kid trying to touch the exhibits
But it'll fade before I get to get a hold of that
Man, I wish I could stop time like a photograph
Every joke that they told I'd know to laugh
Man, man, I wouldn't let a moment pass…

I have discovered myself during my adult life in the UK, more or less. I have had a pretty exciting time on this island. I discovered the British people's addiction to saying "Goodbye" in this tightly knitted, small group, and in the strangest moments people say goodbye. For example, leaving the office or to the cashier in the store. Isn't it awesome? When I began my internship, I was shocked when a farewell party took place. "This isn't farewell. It's just a 'See you later'. That made me realise that you never really say goodbye to anyone, and I still like to use that phrase.

I have always found it worthwhile but awkward to say goodbye. In such situations, the idea of going away as soon as possible is a priority. Allow me to reiterate the opening statement of this chapter in my life: "My people, no goodbyes to you, I'm just gonna say good night." The lyrics from one of my favourite Kanye West songs used to ring through my eardrums whenever I travelled as a child, staring out the window of the plane and seeing all the flashing lights below passing. Apparently Kanye was sampling one of the greatest Dickens novels of all time, *Great Expectations*: "I don't know when we may meet again, and I don't like Good-byes. Say Goodnight!" Whatever was intended, it resonated with me so well. The feeling of saying goodbye sounds too much like a permanent action, something any global nomad who has had the unfortunate destiny of cutting close ties while moving to a new place has experienced.

I didn't entertain such farewell emotions. After probing my mind, I'm pretty sure a counsellor would deem me a psychopath. However, allow me to clarify before I'm pigeon-holed! I never experienced a deep feeling of emotional transparency. For as long as I can remember, I have never shared my problems and emotions with my guardians (father, mother, or maid). Perhaps it sounds like a masculine shell that I have wrapped in layers of heartfelt remorse, but I could not communicate more deeply because I held everything in. I had matured as my parents were travelling, I had and taught myself what independence meant, but my feelings at the time were disconnected and I didn't have a clue what it really meant to be independent. What I thought it meant was the complete opposite to what it really was.

In all this, I felt very inhumane around saying goodbye, and at the same time, ruthless. This has led me to believe that my development has caused my world to be drawn as a 'noir playbook'. Not one week goes by when I don't replay this moment at least once in my head, wondering whether I could have done things differently.

What was this moment? It was my father's funeral. He had two open casket funerals, one in England and the other back home in Zambia – I call this 'home', as that's what my grandmother had asked – for him to be returned home. During both funerals I made a conscious decision not to look at his body, not even once. I cannot tell you what my father looked like, nor what he wore. Do I sound like a psychopath yet? Have you had enough of walking through my psyche? If not, allow me to explain why

Two things ran through my mind as they opened his casket both mornings. The first was: don't cry, be strong for your brothers. The other: I'll see you again, this isn't goodbye. My father and I had a long-distance relationship for my entire life. Most of our conversations would happen over chat platforms such as MSN (popular at the time). Whether he was in Nicaragua, India, Cambodia, or the many places his job took him, we always found a way to speak. I taught myself how to track a human being in another country using phones, and even though the bill would come back in the hundreds, he was never mad. It was as if he was challenging me to find him… and so I always did.

Fast forward to his open-casket funeral. All those memories flooded back to me at once. While looking away from the casket, all I could think about was when I would be given the opportunity to find him again.

As a TCK, or as a globalized nomad tribe, we must know that suffering is real and a part of human existence. It's good to feel sorrow. The hearted agony of goodbyes have to be embraced in order to enjoy the joys of hellos and their connections.

I hated goodbyes, and to this day hate the remains of my youth's traumatic farewell. Nevertheless, I still face them, because it's part of the relationship-stimulus journey. How can we know that we will feel the full extent of being vulnerable to developing relationships without experiencing pain at the last minute for those we value? Pain is a miserable feeling, but we miss the wide range of life and relationships without it. How do we know that we are alive without pain? The next time you find yourself dreading goodbyes, consider how your last goodbyes can prepare you to embrace your next hello.

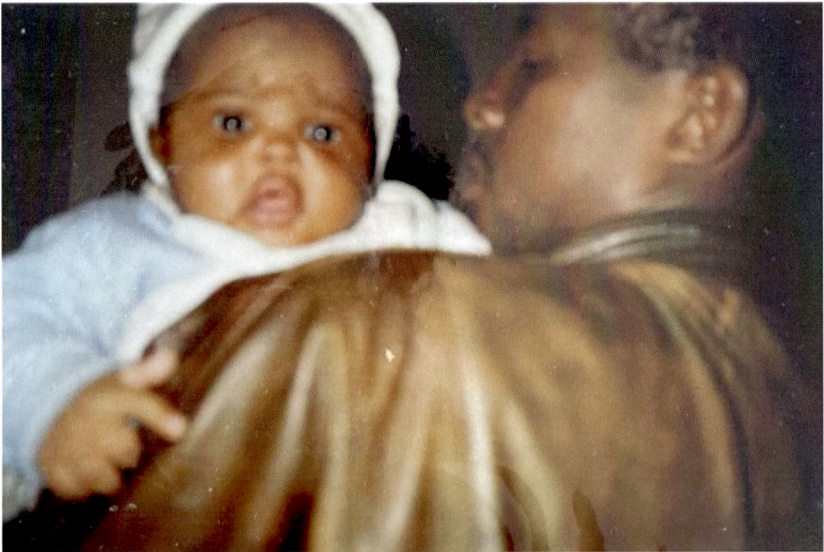

Raymond Pelekamoyo (1992) with my father Victor Pelekamoyo

CHAPTER SEVEN

If you're brave enough to say goodbye, life will reward you with a new hello.
Paulo Coelho

I wanted to share this open letter that addressed kids from the third culture worldwide, saying goodbye to the past. I feel at this moment that the words of a mother with four young third-cultural children should be shared:

> Goodbye. We get a lot of practice saying it. We've said goodbye to short-term workers. They never planned to stay, but we welcomed them into our lives anyway. We've said goodbye to others – longer-term workers whose time in this country has also come to a close for various reasons.
>
> And then, every year, I watch the graduating high school seniors. The ones who leave their families behind and travel to their passport country for their university years – and beyond.

As I write this, all four of you are more than eight years away from entering your college years. Still, someday I will say goodbye to each of you in turn. My oldest son first, then a couple of years later, my youngest son. A couple of years after that, I will be saying goodbye to my oldest daughter. The next goodbye will be my last. My youngest daughter will leave too.

I must say goodbye to you like this, no matter where in the world I live. And when you do leave, there are things I want to tell you. Things like…

You are my child. You are now an adult, and I'm proud of who you are, but you will always be part of my family. Our home can always be your home. No matter where we live, we will always welcome you into it.

We have endeavoured to give you as a stable home life as possible in the ever-shifting international community in which we live. I am sorry for the consistent, repeated, prolonged, never-ending goodbyes you have endured. So, say goodbye well. For many of your high school friends, the goodbye may be forever. You might return to Cambodia; you might not. And your friends may not. Even if they do, it most likely wouldn't be at the same time as you. So honour your friends with good goodbyes...

… Try to live your life in real-time, with real people. Don't waste your time getting drunk, playing video games, or looking at trashy pictures on the internet. That stuff doesn't satisfy me. But even if you do turn to those things, your Papa and I will always welcome you with open arms. We are always your family. Our hearts are open. Our home is open. Possibly more importantly right now, though, is that our inboxes are always open.

And whatever happens, you must know that your Heavenly Father will always welcome you Home. He is always there for you. He will forgive anything. And should you ever stray from Him, don't stay away forever out of fear that He doesn't want you. He wants you. Believe it.

All my love, Mom

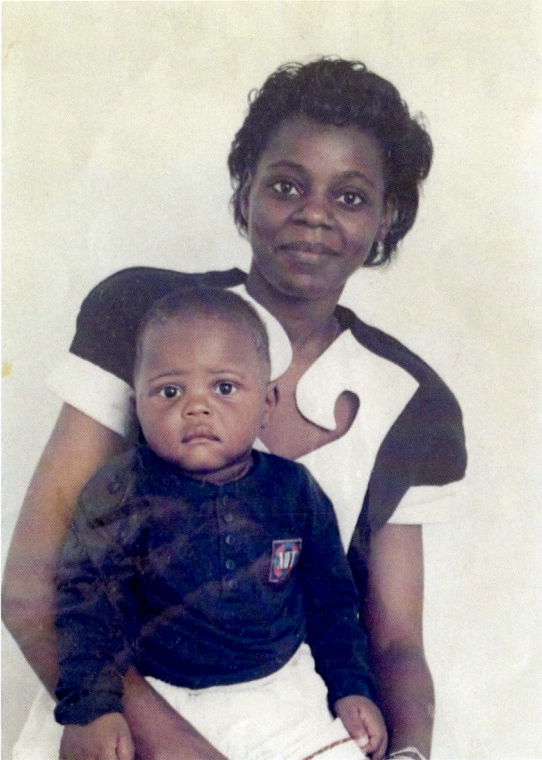

Raymond with my mother Maureen Bwalya Pelekamoyo in 1993, Zambia

Raymond in Harare at a weekend gathering with Oxfam employees

Chapter Eight

No generation before now has had so many of its members simultaneously living in, between, and among countless cultural worlds as is happening today.

Lois Bushong

I was raised by several different members of my family, from my auntie to my uncle, and to my cousins from both sides of my family tree. I mixed between branches and roots so well that I was able to camouflage cultures and blend between the tribes. What I found most fascinating about being raised by different people were the stories I got to hear – from religious stories to the local gossip, and even conspiracy theories.

The person that loved to tell me stories the most was this man that used to visit my grandfather's house in Lusaka. He was a grey-haired man with the longest soft beard you would have ever seen, so large that you couldn't see parts of his face, just the outline of his eyes, nose, and thin lips. Whenever I bumped into him, I would always get shivers as I was slightly scared of him. His eerie presence would send a cold breeze along my neck. His voice had an unusual crackly sound to it, which always appeared when he told his long-winded stories. I never really asked who this man was or why he always turned up at my grandfather's house. He was like a part of the furniture. He never moved, just simply stared at the wall in front of me. It was as weird then as it sounds writing it now.

Anyway, what I remember the most about him was his incredible ability to believe his own stories. For example, he believed that the Chinese were taking over Zambia to re-enslave us, hence the increase in Chinese nationals. Imagine a man in his sixties telling a 12-year-old child this. I just used to nod my head as if I understood what he was talking about. He always used to say, "If we are not careful, there won't be any more black children running around the streets."

As I reflected on what he said, I only began to understand more what he meant when I observed for myself greater freedom of movement within societies throughout the world. I realised that this was in fact globalization, a word that I became familiar with during my time at university. After centuries of technological progress and advances in international cooperation, the world is more connected than ever. Globalization is the word used to describe the growing interdependence of the world's economies, cultures, and populations, brought about by cross-border trade in goods and services, technology, and flows of investment, people, and information.

It struck me like a shell then and has remained with me ever since. I realized that maybe what makes me question my perception of where home is the idea that home doesn't want to adjust to fit the new me. It's the idea that home isn't what it is in the eyes of everyone living there. In the same way, everyone isn't comfortable with the arrival of a huge international corporation landing in their community.

My experience of homes – the ones I have lived in – I wouldn't call them home. They may have had the characteristics of what make up a home, but to me home isn't just a physical space.

In all honesty, I am not shocked. People want the places in which they live to match the mental box they have constructed. However, I also know that your reality is part of the art of self-exploration – it's a world you have created with broken fragments from your subconscious, stored for so long in your mind.

The ideas of globalization have been somehow obscured in this mental box, which we relentlessly seek to introduce. Integration among countries is the central essence of globalization, and the development of the TCK as a term reflects in many ways the increasingly globalized world in which we live. For the past 20 years globalization has been a defining force in the modern global international climate. It has affected all facets of society, loosely characterized as the growing interconnectedness between economies, technology, connectivity, and culture – four things have shaped my life. Isn't that strange, the characteristics of globalization that are defined as bringing people closer together are also the themes of this book that I feel have created this sense of alienation in my own personal life.

So, what does this all mean? In simple terms, the number of people living abroad continues to increase with the growing globalization and its acceptance as a working theory. More research is taking place on the consequences of leaving home countries and the challenges this poses to identity formation and feelings of belonging. This applies to refugees, asylum seekers and normal employees.

Globalization is also considered a one-way street in which other nations are 'invaded' by Western chains. In the West, we still talk about how other places are ruined. Yet I don't believe we should see globalization as 'ruining' a place. The same process that has brought unfamiliar cultures to us has also brought parts of our culture to them.

When you have more cultures interacting with each other, you get to understand that everyone is a human being and shares the same wants and needs.

So, given that people can feel dislocated whether they are left behind or swept up, what separates those who see globalization negatively from those who see it positively is how they perceive changes to their country. Those who are more locally or nationally rooted tend to see globalization breaking down the national community and changing what it means to be part of the nation-state in ways they deem to be negative. In contrast, those who embrace globalization tend to focus on the ways in which globalization itself can create community, fostering new connections by breaking down boundaries between people and increase international cooperation and understanding.

Raymond on left, Victor Pelekamoyo (my father) on the right in Harare, 1998

CHAPTER NINE

Growing up I was always reminded of the importance of community building – being brought up immersed in African culture, it was very evident in my day-to-day tasks. You see, in ancient Africa there was significance in the way that people treated each other in their tribes. Belonging to a tribe meant much more than just a language, it was a support network and the backbone to ensuring collective progress.

This idea of supporting each other through humanity is called 'Ubuntu', an ancient African phrase that is still heavily used across Africa. Surprisingly, the phrase never came up during my upbringing in the United Kingdom, not even once. However, I was introduced to a similar phrase – 'Cogito, ergo sum' – which translates into English as, 'I think therefore I am', which forms the foundation of Rene Descartes' philosophical arguments. Now, if we break down the meaning of 'Ubuntu', it quite literally translates to, 'I am what I am because of who we all are'.

Comparing both phrases we can see how their meanings differ – the western belief focuses on oneself, a very dark and lonely meaning to life, compared to the ancient African focus on community and relationships.

When I look back at my childhood I clearly see the importance that

'Ubuntu' has had on me, especially when making decisions. Would I have fundraised for Haiti if I had not been brought up with the key principles of community building and humanity? Ultimately, I believe that life is always more beautiful when you get to experience it with others, rather than alone, and if this can be combined with collective group development then more people can overcome any troubles that may come their way.

In the case of the Haiti disasters, I always found happiness in the thought that the money we fundraised made its way there and eventually did help someone. I may never know or ever meet that someone, but when I hear stories of people rebuilding their lives in Haiti, it warms my heart.

Over ten years ago, on 12th January 2010, when Haitians started their day they could not have imagined the devastation that was about to befall their country. Later that day, a 7.0 magnitude earthquake struck, claiming the lives of nearly a quarter of a million people. The quake – one of the deadliest natural disasters on record – destroyed much of the country's fragile infrastructure and left many Haitians in dire need of assistance.

I was 16 years old when this happened, a boy in the searching phase of his life, wondering what door would open in the next chapter of his life. I remember walking into school that day as the mood was like a funeral. We could feel the pain that the world was feeling at that exact moment, and there was nothing we could do about it… or that's what we all thought. So, I marched into my school library to procrastinate, but before I could take a seat, I received the best news I could ever dream of – a once-in-a-lifetime trip to train and perform contemporary ballet in Russia. Imagine, the day the world stood still and hundreds of thousands of lives were ruined, I was offered a prestigious invitation to continue my dreams.

My heart sunk. If ever there was a sign that I was a small organism in an unpredictable and engineered world, then this was it. I was so far from the truth. I had never been so blinded to what the rest of the world was going through, and I made it my mission that morning to change that. I must have been crazy (or didn't have my breakfast that morning), and I gave myself the task of funding my trip to Russia, as well as finding a way to do anything to help the people of Haiti.

As I sat down with a friend of mine, a short, dark-skinned boy I'll call Ben sat down in front of me and asked me what I was writing. I took a deep breath and shared my thoughts. He looked at me as if I had just unloaded the weight of the world onto him. The only thing I had managed to write in my book was the word 'dance', together with the reasons I danced. I kept scribbling it down over and over again. One sentence popped up and I had to write it down: 'I dance to make people happy'.

Right there and then I knew what I had to do. I had to dance or find a way that dance could raise people's spirits and help them to believe in themselves, that they could make a difference. We sat down for hours in that library and had endless amounts of snacks, although I should add that Mrs English, the librarian, was not too pleased. Then we finally had the idea – a variety show called, 'I Dance 4'. Without any experience in hosting or producing events, we knew we had to simply wing the entire show.

So, we called every radio station and newspaper, and booked the main school. We gave ourselves four days to arrange it all, but with no idea how our marketing was going, we started to get nervous. The night before the event I stumbled across a social media platform called 'Facebook'! I wasn't entirely sure how it worked or who was on it, but I plastered our event on a local city's Facebook page. We even managed to get a local ice cream company to supply free ice cream.

I would be lying to you if I said I wasn't anxious. We had only managed to sell about 45 tickets, but the hall had a capacity of 250.

At that moment I was nervous not because I had my name on it, but because I felt that I hadn't done enough and this would be an embarrassment. This is why people don't listen to young people, I thought.

4.00 pm arrived and I remember walking to my school after changing out of my uniform when I saw the ten dance schools that I had invited waiting eagerly to enter the building. My inexperienced self forgot that we might need to collect everyone's music and do a technical rehearsal to make sure that the entire event ran smoothly. I was way out of my depth and comfort zone.

Luckily, my dance teachers were experienced and took control, helping this young 16-year-old. During the rehearsals I took a phone call from the local newspaper asking if they could attend, and as I stepped outside to find a quiet area to talk, I was bombarded by crowds of people! I took a step back to look – I couldn't believe what I was seeing. There was the largest queue I had ever seen in my life. It felt as if the entire school and town had shown up. I swallowed my saliva and took a deep breath as I heard a voice on the phone asking me, "Is it going to be a good turnout?"

The show was a success and we had managed to break the 350 capacity. Writing this now still gets me excited as the memories flood back. Just before I walked onto the stage to thank everyone, I was told that we had managed to raise over four thousand British pounds. Before I could say anything, someone's mother shouted at the top of their voice, "We wouldn't have come if it wasn't for you, so thank you!" I never really considered how that sentence may have changed who I was, and how it created an entirely new opening for me.

I stood there holding the cheque in front of the crowd. We had done it. This money was going to be used to help pay for equipment and labour to begin rebuilding parts of Haiti that had been devastated. Before leaving the stage, my headmaster held another cheque out and said, "And to show you our appreciation, here is the £400 you needed for your trip to Russia." In the midst of the chaos and the goosebumps, I had forgotten the other reason why I was dancing!

Many have wondered how I got to where I am. Well, following the success of 'I Dance 4', I was approached by one of the largest communications companies in the world, worth over a billion dollars – a big deal back then. They offered to invest in my idea when I was only 16. After turning them down and focusing on my own passion, I ultimately accepted the offer a few years later when I went to university. 'I Dance 4' became 'The Dance Company' and went nationwide in the UK, as well as having a global footprint. We helped people realise why they danced, and this led me on my journey to being awarded 'Enterprising Individual of the Year' for my work highlighting the troubles developing communities around the world face.

The more I tapped into my own personal insecurities and experiences of being a global nomad, the more I swam in my own untapped potential. Everything after I Dance 4 has been about connecting communities and individuals, about the power of networking. Now I'm in my late twenties, turning 30 soon – t rust me, I am certainly not (and don't feel like) a 16-year-old boy anymore. Whilst I stare at my bedroom desk and I look at my 'Business of the Year Award' and 'Entrepreneur of the Year Award' collecting dust, I still believe there is a lot more work to be done in this world.

A Story of a Survivor

Sa fè lontan

Third Culture Kids are born from different circumstances. Many have been birthed from normal everyday events, but some are brought into this fast-moving world from unusual and unpredictable circumstances. I always reflect on my time as a dancer and how easy it was for me to travel the world with so much freedom. It makes me wonder at times, during black swan events (an event in human history that was unprecedented and unexpected at the point in time it occurred), about the worrying displacement of human beings, something we overlook in our everyday lives. For example, every morning when I watch the early morning news, I am bound to hear stories about people at sea escaping a war-ridden country to seek asylum in another country miles away. The images are very upsetting to say the least, but if I look back at all the TCKs that I have had the opportunity to meet, they all have very similar themes when they discuss their relocation to another country. They all echo similar thoughts and ideas as to why they are where they are. In a nutshell, for most of them (with the exception of children of military parents), it can be simply put down to 'opportunity'.

Guerline Honroe and Oranel Mattelus

The idea that moving somewhere would provide a new start, an escape, an opportunity to become a better person than where they were currently at. So, while many TCKs are born into the name, they are also built and shaped by the environment and consequences that guide them.

Oranel Mettelus and his crew had just finished construction on a home in the wealthy enclave of Pétion-Ville in Port-au-Prince when the earth trembled and brought the structure crashing to the ground. His work collapsed around him, sparing his life but leaving him trapped.

Had Mettelus, then 23, been working in another, less monied neighbourhood, he might have died there. He slept amidst the wreckage until a bulldozer arrived the next day to clear rubble for those residents with connections.

His family was not so fortunate. After Metellus was freed, he picked his way through the debris of his fallen city to reach his own home. It took him two days, instead of the usual hour. He found his house caved in, his parents, three sisters, and three brothers dead inside. Metellus and his one surviving brother, then 15, were alone in a broken city.

"I lived, but it was like a part of me died," he said, ten years later and three hours away from the epicentre and its aching memories. "Everyone who helped and supported me was gone."

Now Metellus is part of Haiti's ongoing efforts to rebuild, working as a mason with WE Charity, a global non-profit. He spends his days constructing para-seismic school buildings that will survive Mother Nature's worst violence, and that in 2010, may have saved his loved ones.

The 7.0 magnitude earthquake that shook the tiny Caribbean nation for 30 seconds on 12th January 2010 killed more than 200,000 and sentenced the country to a rebuilding effort that was dogged by poor governance and spotty aid distribution. Metellus is among the 1.5 million Haitians who were displaced right after the disaster. Many left Port-au-Prince for rural areas, tiny villages whose populations suddenly ballooned beyond capacity, beyond roadblocks and collapsed bridges, farther than most aid supplies reached.

While aftershocks rippled across the country, nearly 100,000 people made their way north from the capital, walking or hitchhiking to safe ground. The world's aid and efforts were focused on the epicentre, where the human toll was greatest. In the Central Plateau region, there was a different type of need.

WE Charity had been working in Haiti for a decade when the earthquake struck, and the organisation zeroed in on its work in rural areas, setting up in Hinche, about three hours from the capital.

On the anniversary of the earthquake, Metellus told his story in Creole through an interpreter, describing his decision to leave Port-au-Prince and travel with a friend who had also lost everything in the capital and wanted to reach family in Kabayi, a small village in the Hinche region: "There was nothing left. We had to move through." When he first laid eyes on Kabayi and surveyed its dirt roads that lead to distant hills in Haiti's only landlocked province, the young man who'd lost everything thought, "I could make something of this."

Guerline Honore had the same thought and had left her home in Mirebalais, a town just outside of Port-of-Prince, for Hinche. She and Metellus had known each other from back home and met up again shortly after leaving. They were already in love, he says, and after losing everything, there was no reason left to deny it or to wait. The couple married and built a house with savings from Mettelus's masonry work and the money made from dry goods Honore sold at the market – rice, pasta, and canned milk.

Metellus picked up odd jobs as a mason and started a family with his wife. When his first son, Michael, reached primary school, his classroom was crumbling. The school building was nearly 90 years

Oranel Mattelus with family.: wife Guerline Honroe, children Michael and Lubens

old, just one room with decaying walls and without a roof. Though Kabayi wasn't hit by the earthquake, after years of neglect the school's condition made it look like it had been.

Metellus tells his story sitting with his two sons, Michael aged six, and Lubens, five. They practice the alphabet in their reinforced classroom, with its para-cyclonic window design that funnels harsh winds through safely, its poured concrete beams at three levels, and its foundation settled deeply into erosion-tested soil. Metellus says he feels stable and secure. There is enough infrastructure here for him to stay. He won't ever go back to Port-au-Prince. In the walls around him, each cinder block had been individually strength-tested – there are around 2,000 of them.

According to their father, Michael and Lubens will be professionals, doctors or engineers, who continue beyond their own Grade 5 education and won't struggle as he did. He walks them to school every day to be sure, even though the trip takes just a few minutes from their home. For now, Michael sings his ABCs softly to himself in his classroom while Mettelus looks on proudly. Soon the brothers will have a sibling; Honore is pregnant with the couple's third child.

As he looks back on that Tuesday in 2010, Mettelus gets anxious. "Sometimes I lay at night and can't sleep at all. I can't stop thinking about it. If my mom and dad were still here, I wouldn't have to figure it out on my own."

He is cautiously optimistic about the future but knows it can be hard to predict. "I'm not sure what tomorrow will bring," he says. "My children are my hope."

We.org. 2020. *Ten years after the earthquake: One survivor's story of fleeing the capital to rebuild.* [online] Available at: <https://www.we.org/en-GB/we-stories/global-development/rebuilding-haiti-ten-years-after-earthquake> [Accessed 15 October 2021].

DONNY'S STORY

My mother and father moved to the London in 1987. My older sister was born in Colombia two years previously, and my other sister was born in 1988. Mother and father moved to London, like many other families, in search of a better life. Fast forward four years and things seemed to be going well for them, until somebody from the casino in Green Park where father was working called immigration. My father was deported as his status wasn't legal at the time. Mother had a choice to make. She had legal status at the time, but as love has a way of doing things, she decided to leave her new life in London to be with father back in Cali, Colombia. Unbeknownst to her, she was already pregnant with me as she boarded the plane.

A few months later after her arrival, I was born in what was the equivalent of a British GP (my sisters joke about this, often at my expense, although I have yet to figure out why!). My parents picked up from where they left off, and legend has it that the whole neighbourhood had been planning a massive celebration in preparation for my arrival, which is so heart-warming to learn. As

Mother and Father arrived back at the house, people were drinking, partying, there were fireworks, and they even hired a DJ! Every time I hear this story, I get goosebumps.

The years went by, life did its thing and my parents inevitably parted ways, due to ongoing issues and differences. About a year or so later, Mother decided to move back to London to rebuild her life, leaving my sisters and me in the care of my grandparents. The year was 1999, I was a six-year-old who was still easily distracted and entertained (I assume, as I do not have many recollections of that year), so not having Mother close by wasn't so painful because I got to live with grandparents, an auntie and eight of my cousins. We lived in a *finca* (Spanish for estate), and we had everything we could wish for – plenty of cousins, amazing food, trees to climb in our backyard, covered in fresh fruit to eat. And the best part – NO SCHOOL!

Mother would call as often as she could and whenever we spoke, I would ask about life in London. For as long as I can remember, I would look at pictures of the double-decker buses that allowed you to hop on and off, the big screens in Leicester Square, Big Ben, the Houses of Parliament and, of course, Buckingham Palace. Life would eventually allow me to see all these places, and later I was even fortunate enough to be personally invited to a Garden Party at the Palace with Prince Charles and Camilla (but that's a story for another time). I can honestly say that Mother's love for London definitely rubbed off on me – she sold it to me so well that I just couldn't wait to join her, despite her constant warnings about the blistering colds she was subjected to! I was simply looking forward to the snow. A whole year later, my sisters and I finally boarded that plane – Mother had saved enough and sent for us, and I was so ready for my new life in London.

We arrived at Heathrow on the evening of 1st July 2000, and there was Mother. She looked so regal to me. I was in such awe at having her stand in front of me that I had forgotten for the moment that I had finally arrived at the place I had always dreamt of going.

It wasn't long before I started my new school, or so it felt like. The first day was magical, and I was so excited to finally put on that uniform and learn! My family joke about the fact that once I got back home from my first day at school in London, I insisted that I had already learnt English. I would say words in Spanish with an English accent. That really sounds like something I'd still say today, to be honest. I was so eager to learn my new language that I was fluent in English in under a year! My teachers, family and the few friends I had at the time were highly impressed. All I ever wanted to do was speak English, so much so that I was the only one to speak English in my house, even though my sisters lived there and had spoken it when they were younger. This made me an asset in my home, as I was appointed to deal with phone calls, dealing with landlords, translating Home Office documents, and even getting myself into the other two primary schools I attended between the ages of seven and ten.

Like every other person walking this planet, this story is complex and gives rollercoaster vibes. There are so many more stories to share and experiences lived that I am beyond grateful to my dear friend Ray for giving me an opportunity to share a glimpse of what life is like as a Third Culture Kid (TCK is a badge of honour I now wear proudly). I met Ray on our way to Berlin in the summer of 2017, outside McDonald's at London Victoria Station. We were the only two males in a group of around 20 and instantly clicked – I guess it was the tattoos. Who knows?

The moment I met Ray I thought he was a very cool dude, unlike anyone I had ever met. From day one he has been an innovator with a mind like no other. This guy has some of the waviest ideas, but above all else he has been like a brother to me since the day we met and he always looks out for me. I wish you all the success in the world, brother.

To many more adventures, laughter and strawberries.

Your brother,

Miguel Gutierrez

CHAPTER TEN

Happiness is not a goal... it's a by-product of a life well-lived.

Eleanor Roosevelt

So, after reading this, you might wonder what it all means. What would you say about yourself in a book with a few words? And if you are one of those who think similarly, your response will be linked to philosophy and theology.

I wish to help you reflect on the thoughts that have arisen as you have listened to the stories shared during this 'fire talk'. Now dear reader, yes you, if you would do me the honour of reflecting with me....

Firstly, be honest with yourself. It's only you, me and your thoughts.

What do I admire in others? In others, what do I admire? What you admire in others is a sign of your worth. The outcome will be greater satisfaction if you apply your ideas to your own life. How much do I enjoy it? Gratitude will help you increase your satisfaction as quickly and as effectively as possible. Take the time to figure out who and what you value. Do I want to be happy or right?

Do you concentrate more on being right, or enjoying the time you have together, when you share with others? Doing the latter will help you to be glad. Am I driven more by fear or passion? Fear involves judgment, concentrating on wrong, resentment, anger, guilt, and shame. On the other hand, passion is focused on hope, ability, appreciation, and a strong desire to concentrate on improving situations. Try to start every day and work from a position of passion instead of fear.

Am I accomplished? You will significantly erode enjoyment by becoming a perfectionist. While the impetus behind your thinking is optimistic, perfectionism is an unobtainable goal that leads to frustration.

Do I influence others positively? You will feel a sense of connection and commitment when you volunteer or simply keep the door open to others. However, do not give too much of yourself, for you lose value in being too accessible. Put yourself first as a priority.

Where do I turn my attention? We frequently concentrate our attention on the past with regrets, or worrying about the future. Try to be present more. And when you think about the past, forgive what has happened and use any difficult experiences as opportunities to improve. Concentrate on what you expect to happen as you think about the future.

How you love yourself is how you teach others to love you.

*Left to right: Epulani (Cousin), Mukuka (late sister),
Raymond Pelekamoyo (me) in Lusaka, Zambia, 1995*

Victor Pelekamoyo, my father

CHAPTER ELEVEN

True belonging doesn't require you to change who you are,
it requires you to be who you are.

Brené Brown

This book is a collection of thoughts and memories used to take the reader through a journey of self-discovery.

Being a TCK is all about the art of self-discovery, self-reflection, and asking a lot of questions. You may even say being a TCK allows you to see the world in a way others may not. I believe that if we were to foster all these unique experiences and bring individuals together, then we could start to create positive dialogue and a movement that would help manage people's anxieties. On the other hand, if the institutions that run our daily lives were to adopt such a mindset, then we would see a much different world from the one we now live in.

I was a four-year-old boy when I first opened my door to a completely different environment, and I was 16 when I used my experience of opening doors to start to create my own door. Would

I have been able to do this without my global footprint or my biological makeup? I'll leave that for you to decide.

In the meantime, if you haven't found *your* key to open *your* doors yet, then maybe the time is now. Or if you are someone who has been opening countless doors, then maybe the time is now for you to start constructing your own door. This entire book was a dream until I opened my eyes. If you keep dreaming about tomorrow, then you will forget to open your eyes and live.

So, what is your purpose?

Where are you really from?

today is going to be a good day

and here's why: because today at least you're you

and that's enough

ACKNOWLEDGMENTS

This book wouldn't have been possible without the individuals and groups – large and small – that allowed me to develop and test insight-related ideas in workshops, masterclasses, or by simply just listening to me.

I owe an enormous debt of gratitude to those who gave me detailed and constructive stories on one or more chapters, including Stephanie Ramesar, Sergeant Nathan Owens, Miguel Gutierrez, Twambo Chinyama, Martin Kalungu-Banda, Neo-Kalungu Banda, Rauni Barros, Dalitso Zimba, Wazani Muwezwa, Ernest Williams, Zavon Miller and everyone on Clubhouse that joined in on TCK discussions. They gave me free time to discuss nuances of the text and pushed me to clarify concepts, explore particular facets, and explain the rationales for specific recommendations.

I'm also immensely grateful to my family, and most importantly to Peter Tyolani Ngoma, for opening my world up to my history and family tree.

I want to also acknowledge Lighton Musdona for sharing the story of how my parents met. A big part of me knows I wouldn't be here if it wasn't for your kindness – thank you.

I want to end by acknowledging key important people that used their own skills and talents to shape this, the finished product. Camron Peters was kind enough to help me design this book – you are the definition of selfless. I've greatly appreciated his counsel during the final stages of completing the book.

To Mrs Russo, thank you for believing in the naughty school kid and making him believe that he is capable of changing the world if only he remembered to dream bigger.

Now… my mother Maureen Bwalya Pelekamoyo, I am deeply indebted to you for everything you have sacrificed for me. I may not show it, but I do love you and home for me will always be where you are.

Finally, last but not least, to my guardian angel. You had such a short space of time to teach me everything you knew. Victor Pelekamoyo, without you this book would never have happened.

BVRSH - #0001 - 211222 - C10 - 210/148/4 - PB - 9781914002243 - Gloss Lamination